Dimitra Eleftheriou-Ernst

GO FOR IT!

Teacher's Resource Book

B1

Hueber Verlag

GO FOR IT! B1
Teacher's Resource Book

Quellenverzeichnis

P. 23: © Thinkstock/iStock/Tanok911
P. 31: Types of holidays, from left to right © Thinkstock/iStock/monkeybusinessimages, © fotolia/Alexander Rochau, © Thinkstock/iStock/AlexBrylov;
Places to live, from left to right © Shutterstock.com/Ron Ellis, © Thinkstock/moodboard, © Thinkstock/iStock/RachelDewis; Types of housing, from left to right © Thinkstock/iStock/bbbrrn, © Thinkstock/iStock/KatarzynaBialasiewicz, © Thinkstock/iStock/monkeybusinessimages;
Ways to communicate, from left to right © Thinkstock/iStock/scanrail, © Thinkstock/iStock/User2547783c_812, © Thinkstock/iStock/thumb
P. 43: tiger, elephant and door: Jörg Saupe, Düsseldorf; plane, book and teacher: Mascha Greune, München; t-shirt: Virginia Azañedo, München; burglar: © Thinkstock/iStock/rod2334; aliens: Beate Fahrnländer, Lörrach; housewife and bank: Michael Mantel, Barum; gorilla: Bettina Kumpe, Braunschweig; football and car: Zacharias Papadopoulos, Athen; wolf: © Thinkstock/iStock/flavioc77; baby: Gisela Specht, Weßling

Bildredaktion: Cornelia Hellenschmidt, Hueber Verlag, München

3. 2. 1. | Die letzten Ziffern
2022 21 20 19 18 | bezeichnen Zahl und Jahr des Druckes.
Alle Drucke dieser Auflage können, da unverändert, nebeneinander benutzt werden.
1. Auflage

Umschlaggestaltung: Sieveking · Agentur für Kommunikation, München
Layout und Satz: Sieveking · Agentur für Kommunikation, München
Verlagsredaktion: Nina Lötsch, Hueber Verlag, München
Druck und Bindung: Friedrich Pustet GmbH & Co. KG, Regensburg
Printed in Germany
ISBN 978-3-19-032940-3

Art. 530_20507_001_01

Contents

	Activity	Use	Focus	Page
Unit 1	**Pleased to meet you!**			
	1 **Have we met before?** whole class; mingling	Classroom activity 4	Asking questions in present simple, past simple, present perfect; *Nice to see you again!*	6
	2 **Explain it, but don't name it** in pairs; game	Classroom activity 5	Lexical field: travelling and talking	8
Unit 2	**Everything was perfect**			
	1 **Travel questionnaire** in pairs / small groups	Classroom activity 1	Asking and answering questions; Lexical field: travel and holidays	10
	2 **An adventure holiday** in groups; discussion and presentation	Classroom activity 6	Discussing holiday options	12
Unit 3	**Keep on learning!**			
	1 **About me** in pairs	Classroom activity 2	Talking about experiences / plans / preferences	14
	2 **A friend's advice** whole class; mingling	Classroom activity 3	Expressing hopes and plans, e.g. the things I would like to change about my current situation	16
Unit 4	**Return to nature**			
	1 **Guess why** in groups; game	Classroom activity 2	Present perfect continuous	18
	2 **Act it out** in pairs; role-play	Classroom activity 4	Present and past participle adjectives; Fluency	20
Unit 5	**What would you do?**			
	1 **Classroom of the future** in groups	Classroom activity 4	Expressing obligation or permission with modal verbs	22
	2 **If I could live my life again ...** in pairs / groups	Classroom activity 5	*If* clause type 2	24
Unit 6	**That's entertainment!**			
	1 **B-movies** in pairs; role-play; individually (writing task)	Classroom activity 2	Talking about films; Writing a short film review	26
	2 **Who wrote it?** in pairs; information gap	Classroom activity 3	Talking about films / songs / books; Statements and questions in passive	28

	Activity	Use	Focus	Page
Unit 7	**It's good value for money**			
	1 **The least interesting type of holiday** in small groups	Classroom activity 2	Comparing things, e.g. different lifestyle options	**30**
	2 **Didn't you?** in groups / whole class; game	Classroom activity 2	Question tags; Guessing reasons / suggesting explanations	**32**
Unit 8	**Life used to be simpler**			
	1 **I used to … but now I …** in pairs; interviewing	Classroom activity 2	*Used to* for past habits	**34**
	2 **Set up your … (but don't say anything!)** in pairs / groups; miming	Classroom activity 3	Understanding instructions on how to use a device	**36**
Unit 9	**Look after yourselves!**			
	1 **Didn't you tell us that …?** whole class; listening comprehension	Classroom activity 3	Using reported speech to ask for clarification; *Didn't you tell us that …?*	**38**
	2 **Ask me politely …** in groups	Classroom activity 5	Making and reacting to polite requests	**40**
Unit 10	**It might be fun**			
	1 **Find the connection** in pairs	Classroom activity 3	Modals of deduction: *could be, might be, must be, can't be*	**42**
	2 **Folk tales** in groups	Classroom activity 5	Understanding / telling a short story; Conjunctions and conjunctive adverbs	**44**
Unit 11	**I don't regret it**			
	1 **Mood meter** in pairs; role-play	Classroom activity 2	Adjectives describing emotions	**47**
	2 **Couples Attack!** whole class; role-play	Classroom activity 4	*If* clause type 3; *I wish … / If only …* + past perfect	**49**
Unit 12	**Time flies!**			
	1 **What will the future bring?** in groups / whole class; role-play	Classroom activity 3	Using *will* for predictions	**51**
	2 **What are you going to do with it?** whole class; mingling	Classroom activity 3	Using *going to* for intentions	**53**

Introduction

This resource book is aimed at teachers working with *Go for it! B1*, teaching English to learners who have already acquired basic knowledge at the A1 and A2 levels. It provides material for 24 communicative classroom activities. In these activities, learners produce the newly acquired language structures in different contexts – this helps them to memorise and eventually use them fluently.

There are two activities for each unit in the coursebook. Each activity corresponds to a specific exercise in the coursebook; it can be carried out directly after the corresponding exercise for consolidation, or later on for revision.

Using the Teacher's Resource Book

There is one page of teacher's notes for each classroom activity: these are comprehensive step-by-step instructions on how to prepare and carry out the activities. They also provide, in some cases, additional ideas on how you can vary or extend an activity according to your students' needs and abilities.

There are various types of activities with different classroom interaction patterns: students interact in pairs, in groups or with the whole class in order to play games, do quizzes, complete info-gap activities, etc. The focus of the activities is on speaking, but the other skills (listening, reading, writing) are practised as well.

Go for it! B1 meets the requirements of level B1 of the CEFR (Common European Framework of Reference for Languages) – in the same way, the activities in this resource book are designed to reflect the communicative situations of the CEFR. Students focus on the corresponding lexical fields, areas of functional language and/or specific grammatical points, and revise them in a light and entertaining way.

To select the appropriate classroom activity for your lesson, look at the table of contents: it shows the corresponding coursebook exercise, the language focus, the type of activity and the classroom interaction pattern. The teacher's notes provide additional information about the activity, such as its approximate duration (since this is dependent on many factors, the times given in the book can only provide a general guideline to help classroom time management).

Further resources for teachers

The *Go for it! B1 Teacher's Notes* (978-3-19-022940-6) provide comprehensive information on working with *Go for it! B1* in class.

You can find further teaching material on the *Go for it!* website at www.hueber.de/go-for-it.

We hope that these resources will help you to add variety to your lessons with *Go for it!* and to respond to the heterogeneity of your student groups.

Your *Go for it!* team

Use	Activity
Unit 1, after classroom activity 4	whole class; mingling
Duration	**Focus**
25–30 mins.	Asking questions in present simple, past simple, present perfect; *Nice to see you again!*

Preparation

Photocopy the worksheet, cut up the cards and shuffle them. If you have a large class, divide it into groups of eight students and make one photocopy for each group. (If you have less than eight students in your class or per group, some students can receive more than one card – but make sure there is a matching partner for each student.)

Procedure

1. Explain the task: students are on a cruise ship somewhere in the Caribbean. At a cocktail party, they see some other guests who seem familiar to them and their objective is to ask and answer questions until they discover if and where they've met these people before. You will give them role cards which have all the necessary information about their new identities and personal histories.
2. Elicit the language students can use to complete the task, for example: *Excuse me, have we met before, you look so familiar!; Have you ever been to … ?; Yes, I have. / No, I've never been there. / I was there in …; Have you ever worked …? / When did you …? / Are you married?; What do you do?; Nice to see you again!* Write some of the phrases on the board (or refer to the functional language in Unit 1). Make sure students have understood your instructions.
3. Before you hand out the cards, make it clear that students should not let other students read their cards. Then hand out the cards, one for each student. They can choose either the masculine or the feminine name on the card. Allow students some time to read their roles and answer any questions they might have.
4. Ask students to stand up, mingle and talk to their classmates to find out whom they have met before, and where.
5. During the activity, monitor and listen carefully. You may want to note down common errors. Assist when necessary.
6. Compare solutions in plenary. If necessary, include a follow-up error correction phase.

Key

Mario / Maria Gonzalez and Paul / Pauline Rutherford met at the University of Hawaii.

Duncan / Debby Lurraby and Jonathan / Joan Smith met at Universal Studios in Los Angeles.

Christina / Christian Jacobs and Robert / Roberta Hunt met at a café in Sydney.

Petros / Petroula Stamatopoulos and Jason Lee / Donna Chen met in Athens, Greece.

Mario / Maria Gonzalez
You were born in Spain in 1972 but have lived in New York City most of your life. Your first job was in 1985 when you worked as an assistant for the law firm Legal and Lethal but you soon found out that the job was not for you. In 2000 you decided to study applied linguistics at the University of Hawaii and now you specialise in teaching children with learning difficulties. You are single.

Paul / Pauline Rutherford
You were born in Hawaii and have spent most of your life there. You are very rich. You were a professional windsurfer but you had a serious accident in 1997 and gave up surfing. Then you decided to change your way of life and see how the "simple, normal people" live so you worked as a cleaner at the University of Hawaii.
You are now married and have a son.

Duncan / Debby Lurraby
You were born in 1982. You almost died in a car accident in 2000 and while in rehabilitation, you met your wife / husband. You got married and moved to Los Angeles, where you pursued a career as an actor. You went to a casting for the film "King of the Kong" but you didn't get the role.
You got to know a lot of famous people, however, and you are still in contact with some of them. You have a son and a daughter who are now studying at the University of California in Los Angeles.

Jonathan / Joan Smith
You were born in San Francisco and you worked as a cameraperson at Universal Studios in L.A. for a long time. Then you started your career as a movie director. In fact, you directed the movie "The Son of Mambo", the second part of the very successful movie "Mambo".
In 2000 you played a small part in the movie "The King of Kong". You played one of the king's men; you died in the first five minutes, unfortunately. You are single.

Christina / Christian Jacobs
You were born in North Africa in 1956 but you moved to Santiago de Chile with your parents in 1970. You studied criminal law and moved to America. You worked as a lawyer at many law firms such as Legal and Lethal in New York City. You didn't like your job very much; however you met nice people there. You've lived with your family in Sydney, Australia, since 1983 and you have your own law firm.

Robert / Roberta Hunt
You were born in Sydney, Australia, and lived there for about 30 years. You moved to L.A. about ten years ago. You left Sydney because you got divorced and you needed to get away from your past life and make a brand-new start. You got a lot of money from the divorce, because you had a very good lawyer who owned his / her own law firm. You think the name was Jacob or something like that. You enjoy your life now with your new partner and you are expecting a child.

Petros / Petroula Stamatopoulos
You were born in Athens, Greece, in 1972 and you still live there.
You are a private detective and you work as a freelancer, mainly for people who want to know if their partners are cheating on them. You think your job is very interesting, and you make good money.
Recently, your job brought you to Sydney, where you followed a man who was cheating on his wife and was on holiday there.
He stayed at a hotel opposite a café close to the opera and you spent a lot of time drinking coffee there.

Jason Lee / Donna Chen
You were born in Singapore in 1960. You moved to Athens, Greece, in 1985 because your wife / husband is Greek.
You have a lot of money so you never needed to work.
A few months ago, you suspected that your wife / husband was cheating on you and you hired a detective to see whether it was true. And yes, it was … unfortunately.
Devastated by the news, you moved to the island of Lesbos, where you have an olive garden. You live a simple, quiet life.

Go for it! B1 Teacher's Resource Book | ISBN 978-3-19-032940-3 |

 Explain it, but don't name it

Use Unit 1, after classroom activity 5	Activity in pairs; game
Duration 15–20 mins.	**Focus** Lexical field: travelling and talking

Preparation

Photocopy the game cards and cut them out (one set of cards for each pair of students).

Procedure

1. Inform students that they are going to play a game, similar to the well-known game *Taboo*™: in pairs, they will take turns explaining a word without using certain 'forbidden' words in their explanations. Give an example if necessary.
2. Hand out the cards: each pair of students receives one set; the cards should be placed face down on a table. Explain that the words written underneath the word in bold are the 'forbidden' words students are not supposed to use.
3. Start the activity and give students about 15 minutes to explain and guess words. The pair that guesses the most words wins.

Extension

In plenary: ask each pair to look up words from Unit 1 and create more game cards. Then ask them to exchange the cards with another pair and play again.

acquaintance know stranger friend	**stranger** friend family colleague
train station train ticket wait	**abroad** country airplane travel
colleague work team office	**personal** data question too
platform train passengers get on	**passenger** train ticket fly
small talk blah blah people weather	**chat** talk friend this and that
get off get on plane go from A to B	**suitcase** clothes carry heavy
airport plane passengers ticket	**culture** country society different

Go for it! B1 Teacher's Resource Book | ISBN 978-3-19-032940-3 | © 2018 Hueber Verlag

Use Unit 2, after classroom activity 1	Activity in pairs / small groups
Duration 20 mins.	**Focus** Asking and answering questions; Lexical field: travel and holidays

Preparation

Photocopy one worksheet for each pair or small group of students. Cut out the cards.

Procedure

1. Inform students that they are going to work in pairs / groups to ask and answer questions about their holiday experiences and preferences, e.g. what their worst holiday was like or if they have ever been on holiday alone.

2. If you think this is necessary, write some question words (or even the beginnings of questions) on the board to help students think of ways to write questions on the topics: *Where …?, How long …?, Why …?, When …?, Who …?, Have you ever …?, Do you like …?*

3. Separate students in small groups or pairs and hand out the cards, face down.

4. Each student draws a card and writes three to four questions about that topic, e.g. *How long was the longest flight you've ever been on? When was it?* They then ask and answer the questions in groups or with their partner.

Extension

You can finish the activity by asking students to report back some interesting travel stories they've heard. You could also ask them to write a short text about one of the stories they've heard as homework.

Longest flight	Worst holiday
Travelling alone	Things you do while travelling
Romantic holiday	Things you miss when you are away from home
Last souvenir you bought	Unforgettable person you met on a holiday
Next holiday	Holiday alone
Favourite person / people you go on holiday with	Famous person you'd like to sit next to on the plane
People you don't like sitting next to on the plane	Something you forgot / found / lost on a holiday

Use	Activity
Unit 2, after classroom activity 6	in groups; discussion and presentation
Duration	**Focus**
20–25 mins.	Discussing holiday options

Preparation

Make one copy of the worksheet for each student in your class.

Procedure

1. Inform students that you are going to give them an advert for adventure holidays; in groups, they will have to discuss the different holidays and decide which one they'd prefer to go on.
2. Put students in small groups of three or four.
3. Hand out the worksheet and if needed, go through the guidelines part with them (on top of the worksheet) to make sure they know what they have to do. Encourage them to make notes so they can tell the class about their plans later.
4. Once you are sure that they have understood their task, start the activity.
5. During the activity, monitor and listen carefully. You may want to note down common errors.
6. After about 15 minutes, groups tell the class about their plans. Allow about two minutes for each group. If necessary, include a follow-up error correction phase.

Extension

Put students in new groups and invite them to think of another destination for an adventure holiday and come up with ideas of what people can do there. They should write their ideas down.
Once they are ready, ask them to present their offer for an adventure holiday to the class. The group that has the best idea wins.

You are a group of friends interested in taking an adventure holiday.
Discuss the possible destinations and decide:

- where to go
- when to go
- how to get there
- what to take with you
- how long you will stay
- what to do when you get there (make a plan)

ADVENTURE HOLIDAYS

DON'T BE BORING! BE FEARLESS!
HAVE A LOOK AT THE FOLLOWING DESTINATIONS AND TAKE THE HOLIDAY OF YOUR LIFE!

WILD CHIMPANZEES AT LAKE TANGANYIKA

- Fly to Lake Tanganyika for the most spectacular safari in Africa.
- Climb the Mahale Mountains and stay in bungalows close to the last wild group of chimpanzees.
- Visit the chimpanzees daily, and stay with them for an hour at a time.

AUSTRALIAN OUTBACK

- Live with the Aborigines and learn how to make and play didgeridoos.
- Meet Aborigine doctors and learn their secrets for good health.
- Meet a famous crocodile doctor and go crocodile hunting!
- See poisonous spiders, snakes and lots of kangaroos!

COLOMBIA

- Work on cocoa plantations and learn from the best.
- Learn about the full cocoa farming process from experts and farmers.
- Help with the packaging and all the paperwork.
- Drink fresh cocoa and learn about cocoa and how useful it is for our health.

NEW YORK CITY

- Discover the other face of New York with an expert guide.
- Stay underground and sleep in empty trains and old metro stations.
- Walk through the tunnels and discover all their secrets!
- If you find something valuable, you can keep it!

Go for it! B1 Teacher's Resource Book | ISBN 978-3-19-032940-3 |

Use	Activity
Unit 3, after classroom activity 2	in pairs
Duration 20 mins.	**Focus** Talking about experiences / plans / preferences

Preparation

Make one copy of the worksheet for each student.

Procedure

1. Inform students that they are going to talk about their personal experiences and plans, for example, about what they have learned, what they would / wouldn't like to learn, where they've been, where they'd like to go, etc. They will have a short conversation about these things with their partner.

2. Give an example and write it on the board, highlighting the target language, e.g.: A: *I've learned to climb. / I'd like to learn inline skating. / I'm not considering learning ice skating because ...* B: *Oh, that's interesting! Why? / Why not? / Go for it! / Sounds great, give it a try!*

3. Pair up students and hand out the worksheets. Allow students about ten minutes to fill in the table with their own answers. Tell them to not only write what they would / wouldn't like to do, but also why.

4. Give students about ten minutes to talk to their partners. During the activity, monitor and listen carefully.

5. Ask each pair to report to the class one interesting thing they have found out, or something they have in common with their partner: *Jan recently learned to climb. He loves his new hobby and he can imagine writing a blog about it. / Hannah and I have both been to Thailand, and we are both thinking about travelling more in Asia next year.*

Knowledge		
I've learned / I've learned to ...	I'd like to learn ... (Why?)	I'm not considering learning ... (Why not?)

Places		
I've been to ...	I'd like to go to ... (Why?)	I can't imagine going to ... (Why not?)

Movies		
I've seen ...	I'd like to see ... (Why?)	I wouldn't like to see ... (Why not?)

Books		
I've read ...	I'm thinking about reading ... (Why?)	I wouldn't like to read ... (Why not?)

Go for it! B1 Teacher's Resource Book | ISBN 978-3-19-032940-3 |

Use Unit 3, after classroom activity 3	**Activity** whole class; mingling
Duration 20–30 mins.	**Focus** Expressing hopes and plans, e.g. the things I would like to change about my current situation

Preparation

Photocopy and cut up the worksheet. Each student needs a slip of paper with "Explain your problem" on the left and "Offer your advice" on the right.

Procedure

1. Inform students that they are going to do a mingling activity to find solutions to their problems and to offer advice on problems their classmates have.
2. Give each student one slip of paper and invite students to complete the sentence under "Explain your problem" with their own ideas. Tell them they don't have to write anything in the cell "Offer your advice"; it gives them an expression they can use to offer their advice, and they will have to improvise the actual advice. Of course, they can use the other expressions from the book, too. Check understanding by performing a mini dialogue with a stronger student.
3. Tell students that reacting after receiving advice is important, too. Elicit phrases that you can use to react to advice and collect them on the board, such as *Great idea! / I'll think about it. / Sounds interesting. / Maybe you're right.*
4. Allow students about five minutes to come up with a problem and write it down on their slip of paper.
5. Once they are ready, ask students to get up and mingle to share their problem with their classmates and receive their advice. Encourage your students to talk to more than one classmate to see whose advice they like best. After they receive some advice and react to it, it's their interlocutor's turn to describe their problem.

Explain your problem: **I would like to meet new people because ______________ ______________.**	Offer your advice: **Have you thought about ...?**
Explain your problem: **I'm tired of ______________ ______________.**	Offer your advice: **Why don't you try ...?**
Explain your problem: **I need a relaxing holiday, but I can't afford ______________ ______________.**	Offer your advice: **Can you imagine ...?**
Explain your problem: **I don't mind ______________ but ______________.**	Offer your advice: **How about ...?**
Explain your problem: **I'd like to ______________ but I can't stand ______________.**	Offer your advice: **Do you like ...?**
Explain your problem: **I'm thinking about ______________ ______________.**	Offer your advice: **Do you enjoy ...?**
Explain your problem: **I feel a bit down about ______________ ______________.**	Offer your advice: **Are you considering ...?**
Explain your problem: **I can imagine ______________ but ______________.**	Offer your advice: **Maybe you should ...**

Use	Activity
Unit 4, after classroom activity 2	in groups; game
Duration	**Focus**
15 mins.	Present perfect continuous

Preparation

Make one copy of the worksheet for each group of three or four students.

Procedure

1. Group students up.
2. Tell students you are going to give them a list of states or situations a person is in and they will have to think of logical / illogical or funny reasons why they are in these situations. Give an example (on the board): *Mary is tired. She has been working too hard.* Explain why the present perfect continuous is used here: Mary being tired is the result of an ongoing action (*working too hard*) that started in the past. The present perfect continuous is used in this way to explain the effect an ongoing action has on someone or something. You can give more examples if you think this is necessary.
3. Hand out a worksheet to each group and ask each group to decide on a good guess for each situation. They should write down their guesses.
4. Compare answers in plenary. The group that has the most creative reasons to explain the situations wins.
5. Ask each group to think of a few situations on their own and write them on their worksheet. They then give the worksheet to the group next to them, who try to find out what the reasons for these situations are.

Extension

Regroup students. One of the students in each group picks one of the statements on the list and the others ask him / her questions to find out more. For example, if the student picks the statement *My hands are dirty. I've been working in the garden.*, the rest of the group asks questions such as: *How long have you been working in the garden? What have you been doing?*, etc. Encourage students to speak freely and use their own ideas.

Key

Possible reasons (some ideas):

Gary's hands are dirty. He's been working in the garden.

Anna is scared. She's been watching a scary film.

James is stressed. He's been working too much recently.

Claire hasn't got any money. She's been spending too much money on clothes.

Steve has a headache. He's been driving all night.

Henry's clothes are wet. He's been jogging in the rain.

Gary's hands are dirty. He's been ______________________________.
Anna is scared. She's been ______________________________.
James is stressed. He's been ______________________________.
Claire hasn't got any money. She's been ______________________________.
Steve has a headache. He's been ______________________________.
Henry's clothes are wet. He's been ______________________________.
____
____
____
____

Use Unit 4, after classroom activity 4	**Activity** in pairs; role-play
Duration 20–30 mins.	**Focus** Present and past participle adjectives; Fluency

Preparation

Make one copy of the worksheet for each pair of students.

Procedure

1. Inform students that they are going to create a short dialogue between two people. From the worksheet you are going to give them, they are going to choose one character each, a mood for each character, and a topic for discussion. So, for example, they could be an annoyed mother and an embarrassed teenager talking about a surprising letter.
2. Pair up the students. Hand out the worksheet and allow two or three minutes for them to decide on their characters and topic. They should fill in one cell from each column, using the adjectives given on the worksheet or their own ideas.
3. Allow about ten minutes for students to prepare their dialogues.
4. Walk around, monitor and help if necessary.
5. Each pair acts out the dialogue they have come up with in front of the class. The class guesses the mood of the characters in the dialogue and the topic of the conversation.

Extension

Invite students to participate in a class discussion. Ask questions using the target language, e.g. *When are you annoyed / motivated / embarrassed / disappointed? / What do you find annoying / motivating / embarrassing / disappointing?*, etc.
Elicit the language needed to answer the questions and write it on the board, e.g. *I'm annoyed / motivated when ...; I think ... is annoying / motivating.*, etc.

Choose an adjective / mood for each character and an adjective to describe the topic.

annoyed annoying bored boring confused confusing disappointed disappointing
embarrassed embarrassing excited exciting relaxed relaxing surprised surprising

Person A		Person B		Topic of the conversation
A / an ________ scientist		a / an ________ friend		a / an ________ dinner
A / an ________ mother		a / an ________ colleague		a / an ________ letter
A / an ________ artist	talks to	a / an ________ teenager	about	a / an ________ film
A / an ________ celebrity		a / an ________ model		a / an ________ weekend
A / an ________ ________		a / an ________ ________		a / an ________ ________

Go for it! B1 Teacher's Resource Book | ISBN 978-3-19-032940-3 |

Use Unit 5, after classroom activity 4	**Activity** in groups
Duration 20 mins.	**Focus** Expressing obligation or permission with modal verbs

Preparation

Make one copy of the worksheet for each student.

Procedure

1. Warm-up: Ask students to imagine how our reality will have changed 50 years from now. Ask them to give you some examples about cars, driving, work, education, etc.
2. Now inform them they are going to create the rules for a future classroom by using the language on the worksheet you are about to give them.
3. Make groups of three to four students and hand out the worksheets, one for each student.
4. Students start the activity: first they should do some brainstorming and then put down the rules on paper. They can use their books and look at classroom activity 4 again to get some ideas on how to formulate rules. Encourage them to be as creative and imaginative as possible.
5. During the activity, monitor and listen carefully. You may want to note down common errors.
6. Students present their future classroom in front of the class. Start a discussion: who had the most innovative ideas? Would the other students like to have lessons in that classroom of the future?

Extension

If there is enough time, students could think of other changes in technology that might occur in the language classroom ten years from now.

What will the classroom of the future be like?
Think about things such as:

- environmentally friendly classroom
- robot teachers
- a new kind of Internet
- learning from home

Illustration: © Thinkstock/iStock/Tanok911

	are allowed to ...	are not allowed to ...
Teachers		
	have to ...	don't have to ...

	are allowed to ...	are not allowed to ...
Students		
	have to ...	don't have to ...

Use Unit 5, after classroom activity 5	Activity in pairs / groups
Duration 15 mins.	**Focus** *If* clause type 2

Preparation

Make one copy of the worksheet for each pair or group of students and cut out the cards.

Procedure

1. Inform students they are going to have a discussion about what could be different in their lives or what they would do differently if they had the chance to live their lives again.

2. To illustrate this, say (for example) that you bought a car that you are not satisfied with. Tell students, *If I could live my life again, I would buy a better car.* Invite your students to give more examples by asking them, *What about you?* You can write some of the examples on the board.

3. Divide students into pairs or groups. Give each pair or group a set of cards.

4. They place the cards on the table in front of them, then take turns to draw a card and tell their partner or the members of their group what they would do differently if they could live their life again. There is a prompt on each card with an example to help them get going. Encourage students to have short discussions about each card, asking each other, *What about you?*

5. During the activity, monitor and listen carefully. Pay attention to the use of the second conditional and note down common errors for an error correction stage at the end.

6. After about ten minutes, students give a short report to the class about what would be different in their lives if they had the chance to live them again. Did they have anything in common with their partner or in their groups?

my job for example: If I could live my life again, I wouldn't move to Frankfurt for my job.	**my studies** for example: If I could live my life again, I would study marketing.	**my holidays** for example: If I could live my life again, I wouldn't travel to Greece in August because it's too hot there.
my habits for example: If I could live my life again, I wouldn't start smoking.	**my hobbies** for example: If I could live my life again, I would learn diving.	**my skills** for example: If I could live my life again, I would learn Spanish at school.
a personal choice I made or didn't make for example: If I could live my life again, I wouldn't buy an expensive car.	**the city I live in** for example: If I could live my life again, I would move to Berlin.	**a change I made or didn't make** for example: If I could live my life again, I would work abroad for a while.
a chance I took or a chance I didn't take for example: If I could live my life again, I wouldn't buy so many lottery tickets.	**a risk I took or a risk I didn't take** for example: If I could live my life again, I would borrow money from the bank to buy a house or a flat.	**a decision I took or a decision I didn't take** for example: If I could live my life again, I wouldn't take that stressful job.

Use	Activity
Unit 6, after classroom activity 2	in pairs; role-play; individually (writing task)
Duration	**Focus**
35 mins.	Talking about films; Writing a short film review

Preparation

Copy the film descriptions on the worksheet and cut them up. You will need one film description for each student in your class. If you have more students than cards, make more copies. Some students will then get the same film description; this is fine.

Procedure

1. Write "B-movie" on the board and try to elicit from students what it refers to: a low-budget film (*movie* being the American term for *film*) with a simple plot and usually unknown / amateur actors. If you have access to the Internet, you could show students the trailers of some B-movies.
2. Divide the class in half for the role-play. Half the students will be actors in a B-movie, the others will be film critics.
3. Hand out a film card to each actor, and give the actors about five minutes for preparation. They should be prepared to talk about and 'sell' their films to the critics. They could also invent more information about the film's plot or ending to be more persuasive. Meanwhile, the critics think of questions they could ask the actors about their films (they could do this in groups). You can refer students back to the language used in classroom activity 2.
4. Once they are ready, students get together in actor/critic pairs and talk about the films for five minutes. Tell the critics they should take notes, as they will write a review of the film later.
5. Now students change roles: the actors become film critics, and the film critics become actors. Hand out film cards to the new actors, but avoid giving them the same film they have already heard about. Proceed as above (Steps 3–4).
6. After the communicative stage, each student (in their role as film critic) writes a review of the film they've heard about. Give them at least ten minutes to do this (they could also do this at home and bring their reviews to the next class). The film reviews are hung around the classroom; students read the reviews and decide which B-movie they would like to see.

Extension

In groups of three to four, students choose one of the films and invent a trailer for it: they should act out a central scene and write the text for the voice-over. They then perform the trailer in front of the class, with one student dramatically reading the voice-over. If you have confident students who like acting, they will enjoy this activity immensely. In the end, the class can decide which film receives the Rotten Melon Award (an award for the worst film of the year).

ZOMBIE LOVE

A zombie, Jacob, falls in love with a young woman, Anna. Unfortunately, her mother, Larissa, doesn't like him and she does everything she can to destroy their relationship. Jacob tries to find a job and get a normal life, but life is really hard for zombies ... Will Anna and Jacob's love survive death?

A VIKING IN NEW YORK

A Viking, Ragnarok, travels through time and arrives in present-day New York. He is completely lost, and all he wants is to go back to his world! But everything changes when he meets a charming New Yorker, Samantha, who asks him to help her find her lost cat.

THE BIG OUCH

A British family is living happily in a village near the Amazon, when one day a giant mosquito comes out of the jungle! Jack, his wife, Emily, and their daughter, Laura, must do their best to save themselves and the village from the terrible giant mosquito. Will they get away?

AGENT HERLOCK SHOLMES

The famous secret agent Herlock Sholmes has to investigate a very strange case. There is a mysterious hole in the wall of Miss Matheson's apartment. How did it get there? What happened? Why did they call him to investigate?

THE LONELY SHERIFF AND HIS HORSE

A sheriff, Logan, is very tired of catching bad guys and wants to get away from it all. He gets on his horse, Belle, and travels around until, one day, his horse starts talking to him in English! They start a conversation and Logan begins to see his life in a completely different way.

DOGARIAN

A young boy, Jimmy, sees a strange light near his home at night and goes to see what it is. He finds a sweet alien dog with three ears and three eyes! When the dog introduces itself with the words "Hello, my name is Dogarian," Jimmy wonders, "And now what?" What is he going to do with the alien dog? What is he going to tell his mother, Julia, about Dogarian? And will Dogarian stay with him on earth?

THE SINGER WHO CAN'T SING

Mark becomes a very famous singer – even though all of his friends know that he can't sing! How is this possible? Everyone is surprised by his success, including his girlfriend, Jenny. What's Mark's secret?

Use Unit 6, after classroom activity 3	**Activity** in pairs; information gap
Duration 25 mins.	**Focus** Talking about films / songs / books; Statements and questions in passive

Preparation

Make a copy of the worksheet (if you have more than nine students, photocopy the worksheet more than once) and cut it up. You need one set of (facing) paper slips for each pair of students, A and B.

Procedure

1. Inform students that they will work in pairs to talk about popular songs, books and films. They will need to ask their partner questions to find out the missing information.
2. Copy the categories below on the board (see boardscript). Elicit one or more questions for each category (*Song title, Performed by*, etc.). For a weaker class, you can write the question(s) on the board as a reference for students. Then write the answer for each question. Make sure students don't think they have to use the passive form for all of the questions – sometimes, the active form is more natural!

Song title: Candle in the Wind	What's the title of the song?
Performed by: Elton John	Who was the song performed by? / Who performed / sang the song?
Released in: 1997	When was the song released?
Written by: Elton John and Bernie Taupin	Who wrote the song? / Who was the song written by?

3. Put students in pairs. Hand out the slips of paper (one set of two slips per pair of students) and let students complete the missing information by asking each other questions. Give them about ten minutes for this.
4. Students present their song, book or movie to class. Here, most statements would sound most natural in the passive form, as presented in classroom activity 3 (e.g. *The song was performed by …; The film was directed by …; The main character was played by …*, etc.).

Variation

Before presenting their song, book or film to the class, students can try to find out more information about it on the Internet. As part of their presentation, they could show a picture of the book's author, a trailer for the film or a music video of the song on YouTube.

1 Student A Song title: Hotel California Performed by ______ Released in 1977 Written by ______	**1 Student B** Song title: ______ Performed by The Eagles Released in ______ Written by Don Felder, Don Henley and Glenn Frey
2 Student A Song title: Yesterday Performed by ______ Released in 1965 Written by ______	**2 Student B** Song title: ______ Performed by The Beatles Released in ______ Written by John Lennon and Paul McCartney
3 Student A Song title: We Are the Champions Performed by ______ Released in 1977 Written by ______	**3 Student B** Song title: ______ Performed by Queen Released in ______ Written by Freddie Mercury
4 Student A Book title: The Lord of the Rings Written by ______ Published in 1954 Made into a film in ______	**4 Student B** Book title: ______ Written by J. R. R. Tolkien Published in ______ Made into a film in 2001
5 Student A Book title: Out of Africa Written by ______ Published in 1937 Made into a film in ______	**5 Student B** Book title: ______ Written by Karen Blixen Published in ______ Made into a film in 1985
6 Student A Book title: Harry Potter and the Philosopher's Stone Written by ______ Published in 1997 Made into a film in ______	**6 Student B** Book title: ______ ______ Written by J. K. Rowling Published in ______ Made into a film in 2001
7 Student A Film title: Skyfall Directed by ______ Released in October 2012 Main character played by ______	**7 Student B** Film title: ______ Directed by Sam Mendes Released in ______ Main character played by Daniel Craig
8 Student A Film title: Pretty Woman Directed by ______ Released in March 1990 Main characters played by ______ ______	**8 Student B** Film title: ______ Directed by Garry Marshall Released in ______ Main characters played by Julia Roberts and Richard Gere
9 Student A Film title: The Hangover Directed by ______ Released in May 2009 Main character played by ______	**9 Student B** Film title: ______ Directed by Todd Phillips Released in ______ Main character played by Bradley Cooper

Go for it! B1 Teacher's Resource Book | ISBN 978-3-19-032940-3 |

Use Unit 7, after classroom activity 2	**Activity** in small groups
Duration 20 mins.	**Focus** Comparing things, e.g. different lifestyle options

Preparation

Make one copy of the worksheet for each group of three to four students.

Procedure

1. Tell students they are going to find out what they have in common with their classmates. They are going to make comparisons about different lifestyle choices: holidays, technology, accommodation, etc.

2. If you think it is necessary to revise the different ways of comparing things, you could write the words "ebook", "tablet", "book" on the board and start out by saying: "What do you think is the most practical option for reading books, and what's the least practical?" Then collect some arguments in favour of or against one or the other option, for example the fact that ebooks are *less heavy than* normal books and they're *easier* to read on *than* tablets. All kinds of arguments could come up. Try to focus on comparing the three things and, by doing this, to elicit the structures students practised in classroom activity 2c, e.g. *less …, the least …, (not) as … as …*, etc.

3. Divide your students into small groups of three or four and hand out a worksheet to each group. Students look at the pictures and make comparisons, talking as much as possible and giving reasons where appropriate. They should try to agree on a statement in their group about the items they are comparing, for example, *For us, a smartphone is the most practical way to communicate, and a landline phone is the least practical way. / We think a learning holiday is the least interesting type of holiday.*

4. Compare students' answers in plenary. Ask each group what they think about the items on the worksheet. They should try and give reasons for their opinions. Depending on your class, a controversial discussion might ensue where groups try to convince each other.

Variation

A weaker class might need guideline questions for comparing the things on the worksheet. You could tell them, for example, to discuss what the most interesting type of holiday is or the most practical way to communicate. These simple prompts will give students a better idea about the direction in which their discussion should go.

Types of holidays

Working holiday

Learning holiday

Adventure holiday

Places to live

Living in the city

Living in the suburbs

Living in the countryside

Types of housing

Big house

Small flat

Flat share

Ways to communicate

The latest smartphone

Mobile phone

Landline phone

Use	Activity
Unit 7, after classroom activity 2	in groups / whole class; game
Duration	**Focus**
25 mins.	Question tags; Guessing reasons / suggesting explanations

Preparation

Make one copy of the worksheet and cut up the cards. Each group receives one card. If you have a small class, you can give each group more than one card and repeat the activity several times.

Procedure

1. Group up students. Tell them they are going to play a guessing game.

2. Offer students an example. Say *I forgot my keys at home this morning. Why do you think this happened?* Tell students that when you make a guess or suggest an explanation about why something happened, you can use a question tag. Model a possible guess, e.g. *You were in a hurry, weren't you?* Invite your students to make more guesses in the same way. (If students grasp this concept easily, you may want to furthermore point out that asking the question tags with rising intonation denotes uncertainty and asking them with falling intonation denotes certainty.) You can react to their guesses, dismissing any wrong guesses with a short answer (e.g. *No, I wasn't.*) and confirming the right guess, if it comes up (*Yes, I was. / Yes, you're right.*).

3. Hand each group one or more cards and tell them that only one student can look at the card. In the group phase, this student reads out the fact on the card, but keeps the reason to himself / herself. The other students in the group offer an explanation, using a question tag when guessing. The student who read the fact can confirm or dismiss their guesses. Give students up to ten minutes for this.

4. When the time is up, ask the groups to perform their guessing game for the rest of the class. Each guess should be delivered in a convincing way. The rest of the class have to say which guess, if any, they think was right. The student who read the fact needs to confirm this or explain the real reason in the end.

Fact: I rode the underground without a ticket. Reason: The ticket machine was broken.	Fact: Yesterday, I said I'm too ill to go to work, but a colleague saw me in a clothes shop in the city centre. Reason: I needed to ask where the nearest pharmacy is.	Fact: I promised to cook dinner for my partner but I didn't. Reason: The oven was broken.
Fact: I promised to stop smoking but my partner found cigarettes in my pocket. Reason: I bought the cigarettes for a colleague and forgot to give them to her.	Fact: All my clothes were wet when I came home from work yesterday. Reason: I got into a bad thunderstorm on my way home.	Fact: I forgot my keys at home this morning. Reason: I was distracted because my mobile phone rang when I left the house.
Fact: I was at the police station for three hours yesterday. Reason: I wanted to report a crime. Someone stole my laptop.	Fact: I went to bed really late last night. Reason: I was watching my favourite TV series and couldn't stop.	Fact: I don't have money to pay the rent. Reason: I bought expensive tickets to an exotic holiday destination.
Fact: My photo is on the glass door of a super-market with the words "Hero of the Month" under it. Reason: I caught a man stealing crisps.	Fact: My partner found a strange telephone number in my pocket with the initials CS. Reason: "CS" is short for "Customer Services". I called them to complain about a sofa I bought recently.	Fact: I was late for my eight o'clock meeting at work. Reason: My train was late because there was a cow on the tracks.

Use Unit 8, after classroom activity 2	**Activity** in pairs; interviewing
Duration 25 mins.	**Focus** *Used to* for past habits

Preparation

Photocopy the worksheet according to the number of students in your class (the worksheet has role cards for eight students – four reporters and four interviewees).

Procedure

1. Get students in the right frame of mind for this activity with a personal example: tell them about a big change that has happened in your life, e.g. moving to another country, getting married, having children, etc. Write on the board "Then" and "Now", and under those headings, write the language needed for this activity: *I used to ... but now I ...* Give a few examples for each expression, e.g. *I used to see my parents once a month, but now I only see them twice a year*, or *I used to sleep late at weekends, but now I get up at six o'clock every day.* Encourage students to give some examples of their own (but without going into too much detail at this point – they can do that in the extension activity below).

2. Now tell your students they are going to do a role-play in pairs. One of them is a person who has made a big change in his or her life and the other one is a magazine reporter interviewing them about this change.

3. Put your students in pairs and hand out the role cards (two facing role cards on the worksheet form a pair). Tell your students to read the information on the role cards carefully and prepare their questions and answers. Give them about ten minutes for preparation.

4 Give students another ten minutes for the interview. Monitor and listen in, and help if necessary (especially with using the new form *used to* for past habits in the questions and answers).

5. After the interview, the reporters present their interview partner in plenary and report a few things they have learned about them, e.g. *Robert Hudson used to live in a big apartment on Third Avenue, but now he lives in a wooden hut on the beach.*

Extension

Students think of changes that have happened in their lives. They get together in pairs and have a conversation about these changes.

You are a reporter from *Run!* magazine. You are going to interview Jane Woodrow, a woman who used to be a real couch potato but is now preparing to participate in the hardest triathlon in the world, the Ironman in Hawaii. You want to find out:

- what hobbies she used to have before she changed her lifestyle
- what she used to eat and what she eats now
- how often she used to do sports and how often she does sports now

You are Jane Woodrow. A reporter from *Run!* magazine is going to interview you about your life five years ago, when you were a couch potato, and now that you're preparing to participate in the hardest triathlon in the world, the Ironman. You will talk about:

- what hobbies you used to have before you decided to change your lifestyle
- what you used to eat and what you eat now
- how often you used to do sports and how often you do sports now

You are a reporter from *Outdoors* magazine. You are going to interview Robert Hudson. He used to live in New York but recently became the first person to live on Oru-oru, a very small island in the Pacific, where he works as a wildlife ranger. You want to find out:

- what job he used to have in New York and how he used to get to work
- what kind of house / apartment he used to live in and how he lives now
- what he used to do in the evenings in New York and what he does now

You are Robert Hudson, the first person to live on Oru-oru (a very small island in the Pacific). A reporter from *Outdoors* magazine is going to interview you about your old life in New York and your new life as a wildlife ranger on Oro-oru. You will talk about:

- what your job was in New York and how you got to work
- what kind of house you used to live in and how you live now
- what you used to do in the evenings in New York and what you do now

You are a reporter from *Techie trends* magazine. You are going to interview Annabelle Ruthland, who invented and built a robot that does all her shopping, cooking and cleaning for her. You want to find out:

- how she got the idea for the robot and how she built it
- how much time she used to spend on cooking and cleaning and how much time she spends on this now
- how she spends all her free time now

You are Annabelle Ruthland. A reporter from *Techie trends* magazine is going to interview you about the robot you invented that does all your shopping, cooking and cleaning for you. You will talk about:

- how you got the idea for the robot and how you built it
- how much time you used to spend on cooking and cleaning and how much time you spend on this now
- how you spend all your free time now

You are a reporter from *Rich!* magazine. You are going to interview Henry Luckless about his life before and after he won the 35 million euro jackpot in the lottery. You want to find out:

- what his job used to be and if he's still working now
- what he used to do in his free time and what he does now
- how much money he used to spend on clothes, food, travelling, etc., and how much money he spends now

You are Henry Luckless. A reporter from *Rich!* magazine is going to interview you about your life before and after you won the 35 million euro jackpot in the lottery. You will talk about:

- what your job used to be and if you're still working now
- what you used to do in your free time and what you do now
- how much money you used to spend on clothes, food, travelling, etc. and how much money you spend now

 Set up your ... (but don't say anything!)

Use Unit 8, after classroom activity 3	Activity in pairs / groups; miming
Duration 25 mins.	**Focus** Understanding instructions on how to use a device

Preparation

Photocopy and cut up the worksheet. You need one card for each pair or small group of students.

Procedure

1. If possible, bring an MP3 player or other device (and the necessary equipment, such as a USB cable, laptop, etc.) to class and ask your students to tell you how to set it up. Most students will know how to do this, but may struggle with finding the right words in English to describe it. Refer them back to classroom activity 3 in the coursebook to revise a few basic words for the process, such as *unpack, plug in, switch on, turn up / down*, etc. For every step of the setup process your students are telling you about, repeat what they said (e.g. *OK, so you have to plug in the USB cable* ...) and demonstrate each instruction with exaggerated movements.
2. Put your students in pairs or small groups (of three or four). Give each group a slip of paper and tell them they are going to read instructions for more electronic devices. They should read the instructions carefully and think about how they can demonstrate them with movements (i.e. mime them).
3. Once you are sure that students have understood their task, start the activity. Allow about five minutes for preparation.
4. Then have the different pairs / groups mime their instructions. They cannot tell the class what their product is. Tell the rest of the class to take notes and write what they think the different steps in the setup process were.
5. Once a pair / group has mimed the instructions, ask the other students to read out their notes and say what they think the device is. The pair / group confirms any correct guesses and says if the class has figured out what it says on their instruction sheet.

Smartphone

1 Unpack the smartphone and the battery.

2 Insert the battery into the phone.

3 Plug the USB cable in to the smartphone.

4 Connect the USB cable to your laptop to charge the battery.

5 Wait for two hours, then switch on your smartphone.

Mobile phone SIM card

1 Unpack the SIM card from the envelope.

2 Switch off your mobile phone.

3 Insert the SIM card into your phone.

4 Switch your phone on again.

5 Use your new SIM card to make phone calls or use mobile Internet.

Bluetooth headphones

1 Unpack the headphones.

2 Check that all the parts are there.

3 Insert the batteries into the remote control.

4 Press the power button on the headphones.

5 Use the remote control to turn the sound up or down.

Portable hard drive

1 Unpack the hard drive.

2 Check that all the parts are there.

3 Put the hard drive on a flat surface.

4 Plug the power cable in to the hard drive.

5 Connect the hard drive to your computer with the USB cable.

Use Unit 9, after classroom activity 3	Activity whole class; listening comprehension
Duration 15 mins.	**Focus** Using reported speech to ask for clarification; *Didn't you tell us that ...?*

Preparation

Photocopy and cut up the worksheet. Each student needs one slip of paper.

Procedure

1. Tell your students you are going to tell them a story about a couple. Tell them to imagine you told them the same story yesterday, and that since you are a bit tired today, you might mix up some details.
2. Give students the worksheets and tell them that these are some facts from the story you told them yesterday. Give them about five minutes to read through and familiarise themselves with the sentences.
3. Tell students to pay close attention to the story as you tell it now, and to interrupt you and correct you if you say something different from what's on their worksheets. They should start with "Excuse me, but didn't you tell us that ...?", then include the corresponding statement from their worksheet. The aim is for students to spot as many mistakes as possible.
4. Tell students the story below. (The information that is different on the students' worksheets is in italics, and you could emphasise the 'wrong' sentences in your story.) If you tell the story from memory, the whole situation will seem more realistic.
5. Every time a student interrupts you and corrects you, praise them for their good attention, and correct yourself: "Oh, of course, you're absolutely right. Daniela *is* in her thirties."
6. In the end, you could have a discussion about what students think actually happened. (One answer might be that Daniel is planning to propose to Daniela: he talks to a wedding planner, then buys a beautiful engagement ring. The limousine will take him and Daniela to a romantic place where he will propose.)

Daniel and Daniela – the perfect couple?
Daniel and Daniela seemed like the perfect couple. Daniela is *in her twenties*, has a great job, and a lot of friends – the same as Daniel. Daniel likes surfing, dogs, and going to the cinema. He *doesn't have a lot of money*, and a lot of women think that's very attractive, but Daniela doesn't care. She likes the simple things, like swimming, going for walks, playing *with her two dogs* and watching films.
They met *at an after-work party* and couldn't stop talking the whole evening. Two days later, they *had a romantic dinner together* and saw a different film, and after that you never saw one of them without the other. They have been together *for five years* now, but lately, there seem to be problems. Daniel started having secrets. A friend of Daniela's saw him *with an elderly lady* who said to him: "I hope you found a good excuse to get away from Daniela." Another friend saw him in a bar one day. He was talking to a stranger and seemed very *angry*. The stranger said to him: "You will pay in cash, so nobody will know." And still another friend of the couple overheard Daniel on the phone. He was ordering *a wedding cake*. What on earth does Daniel need *a wedding cake* for?!
Daniela is *angry* when she hears about Daniel. She doesn't know what's going on with Daniel, and she's afraid to ask.

Daniel and Daniela – the perfect couple?
This is what your teacher told you about Daniel and Daniela yesterday:

Daniela is in her thirties.
Daniel has a lot of money.
Daniela likes playing with her two cats.
Daniel and Daniela met at a film festival.
Two days later, they went to the festival again.
They have been together for two years.
Someone saw Daniel with a beautiful young woman.
Someone saw Daniel in a bar and he seemed very nervous.
Daniel ordered a limousine.
Daniela is worried when she hears about Daniel.

Daniel and Daniela – the perfect couple?
This is what your teacher told you about Daniel and Daniela yesterday:

Daniela is in her thirties.
Daniel has a lot of money.
Daniela likes playing with her two cats.
Daniel and Daniela met at a film festival.
Two days later, they went to the festival again.
They have been together for two years.
Someone saw Daniel with a beautiful young woman.
Someone saw Daniel in a bar and he seemed very nervous.
Daniel ordered a limousine.
Daniela is worried when she hears about Daniel.

Daniel and Daniela – the perfect couple?
This is what your teacher told you about Daniel and Daniela yesterday:

Daniela is in her thirties.
Daniel has a lot of money.
Daniela likes playing with her two cats.
Daniel and Daniela met at a film festival.
Two days later, they went to the festival again.
They have been together for two years.
Someone saw Daniel with a beautiful young woman.
Someone saw Daniel in a bar and he seemed very nervous.
Daniel ordered a limousine.
Daniela is worried when she hears about Daniel.

Use Unit 9, after classroom activity 5	Activity in groups
Duration 20 mins.	**Focus** Making and reacting to polite requests

Preparation

Photocopy the worksheet and cut it up. Each group needs ten cards; for larger classes, make more than one copy of the worksheet.

Procedure

1. Inform students that they are going to have short conversations in groups in which they politely ask a member of their group to do something.

2. Remind students how to ask for something politely (refer to Page 134 in the book). Elicit typical phrases to ask for a favour politely and write them on the board as chunks, e.g. *Can you ...?, Could you ...?, Do you think you could ...?, Would you mind ...?* In the same manner, collect phrases to react to polite requests, e.g. *OK, no problem., Yes, of course., Sure., I'm sorry, but ..., I'm afraid I can't ...*

3. Demonstrate the use of the target language with a student by asking them for a favour, for example, *Could you open the window, please?* Encourage the student to answer, doing what you've asked them to do or politely declining your request. If they don't want to do you a favour, they have to invent a reason why.

4. Divide the class into groups of three to five and give each group ten cards. The groups put the cards face down on their desk. In turns, students take a card and read it. Then they ask someone in their group to do what it says on the card – they have to make sure to not simply use the imperative form on the card, but to formulate a polite request, as you practised in plenary before. The other person has to either do what they've been asked for or politely decline the request. If they decline the request, they have to give a reason why.

Extension

Students form new groups and discuss which of the requests they would fulfill and for whom; e.g. would they give 1000 euros to a family member in need, or a friend? What would be the conditions? In what circumstances would they buy someone a plane ticket to New York (e.g. as a wedding present)?

Give me 1000 euros!	Stand up and sit down three times!	Open the window!	Count backwards from 49 to 39!
Say the alphabet backwards from Z to F!	Spell your name starting from the end!	Shout out your name!	Pretend you're a chicken!
Give me your shoes!	Lend me your car!	Buy me flowers!	Buy me a plane ticket to New York!
Close the window!	Stand on one foot for ten seconds!	Scratch your right ear with your left hand!	Cook dinner for me!
Tell me a joke!	Draw a horse on the board!	Give me the keys to your house / flat!	Give me your home address!

Go for it! B1 Teacher's Resource Book | ISBN 978-3-19-032940-3 | © 2018 Hueber Verlag

Use Unit 10, after classroom activity 3	**Activity** in pairs
Duration 15 mins.	**Focus** Modals of deduction: *could be, might be, must be, can't be*

Preparation

Make copies of the worksheet and cut it up. You will need one card per pair of students.

Procedure

1. Inform students they are going to hypothesise about how two things might be connected. To demonstrate this, write the words *a book – a fly* on the board, and model some ideas, e.g. *The fly could be stuck in the book. The fly might be trying to read.* (You may want to write *could be, might be*, etc. as chunks on the board.)

2. Encourage your students to react to your theories (e.g. *No, that can't be, flies don't read,* etc.). You should write more chunks on the board, such as *can't be, must be,* so that the students have enough input to work with. Make sure that all hypotheses are in the present tense (students don't know yet how to make deductions for the past, such as *must have been*, etc.).

3. Put students in pairs and inform them that you are going to give them a card with pictures of two apparently unconnected things and they will have to come up with logical or absurd explanations or hypotheses about how the two things might be connected. Tell them to react to any theory their partner puts forward, e.g. *No, the … can't …*, or *Yes, the … must / could …* In the end, they should agree on a theory together.

4. Hand out one card from the worksheet to each pair. Allow about five minutes for them to talk in their pairs.

5. Pairs then take it in turns to tell the class about their two things and how they are connected, for example: *We have a tiger and an airplane. We think that the tiger must belong to a magician who is flying from Africa to the USA to show his magic trick 'The tiger that turns into a kitten'. The tiger might be kept in a cage in the cargo area of the airplane.* Then have a class vote on the best story.

Extension

Students change partners. Invite them to each put a personal item on their desk (even a receipt would suffice). Their partner then speculates about their personal item: *I can see on your receipt that you bought vegetables – you must like eating healthy food. / You bring your e-book reader when you come to class – you must have a long trip to get to the language school.*

Illustrations: Tiger, elephant and door: Jörg Saupe, Düsseldorf; plane, book and teacher: Mascha Greune, München; t-shirt: Virginia Azañedo, München; burglar: © Thinkstock/iStock/rod2334; aliens: Beate Fahrnländer, Lörrach; housewife and bank: Michael Mantel, Barum; gorilla: Bettina Kumpe, Braunschweig; football and car: Zacharias Papadopoulos, Athen; wolf: © Thinkstock/iStock/flavioc77; baby: Gisela Specht, Weßling

Use Unit 10, after classroom activity 5	**Activity** in groups
Duration 25–30 mins.	**Focus** Understanding / telling a short story; Conjunctions and conjunctive adverbs

Preparation

Make photocopies of the two worksheets and cut them up. You need one worksheet for each group of students in your class.

Procedure

1. Tell your students they are going to read a special kind of story: a folk tale. Clarify what that is (an old traditional story typically passed on by word of mouth) and ask your students if they know any folk tales in German or in their native language (if they mention a tale that also exists in English, you can tell them the English name for it).
2. Tell your students they are going to work in groups and put together different pieces of a folk tale. They will also have to complete the tale by filling in a few missing words which they will find on an extra slip of paper.
3. Put your students in two groups. If you have a lot of students in your class, you can make four groups and give two groups the same tale.
4. Hand out the cut-up tales to the groups. Give them about 15 minutes to fill in the missing words and put the stories in the right order. In the end, tell them to find a suitable title for their tale.
5. Students tell their tale to the class. They should try not to just read the different parts of the tale, but to retell it. If more than one group has worked with the same tale, tell the first group to mention only what happens in the first one or two paragraphs and let the other group(s) tell the rest.

Extension

Students look up more folk tales online – they could do this as a direct follow-up to the activity, if there is time, or as homework. In both cases, their task is to tell the story to the class, without the resolution. The class then tries to guess the end of the story.

Key

(Possible answers)

Worksheet 1, from left to right: Many years ago, Suddenly, Finally, unbelievably

Worksheet 2, from left to right: Unbelievably, Immediately, finally, it turned out that unbelievably many years ago finally suddenly

____________________, there was a young man who was very sad because he worked and worked, but he had no money. One day, he decided to go to the High Mountain to ask the Wise Old Man why this was so. The journey was long and he was very tired, when luckily, he saw an old house next to the road. An old woman came out and he said to her, "I'm going to the High Mountain to ask the Wise Old Man a question. Could I stay here for the night?" The woman agreed and offered him some food. Before he left the next morning, she asked, "Would you please ask the Wise Old Man a question for me? I have a beautiful daughter, but she never laughs or smiles. Can you please ask him why?"

"I will," promised the young man immediately, and left. When he was very close to the High Mountain, a great river blocked his way. "How can I ask the Wise Old Man my questions if I can't cross the river?" he said to himself.
____________________, a big dragon came out of the forest and said, "You are going to see the Wise Old Man? Can you ask him a question for me? I have always lived a good and quiet life but I cannot fly up to heaven. If you ask him about this, I will help you cross the river."
"I will," promised the young man again and the dragon helped him cross the river.

____________________, the young man arrived on the High Mountain and stood in front of the Wise Old Man. He said, "I would like to ask you three questions." "Wait," said the Wise Old Man. "Unfortunately, you can only ask two questions. You have to think very carefully about which ones you are going to ask." The young man didn't know what to do: he had promised the dragon and the old woman to ask their questions, but he also wanted to ask his own question. So first, he asked about the old woman's daughter who never smiled, and the Wise Old Man said, "She will smile – when she meets the man she will marry." The young man thanked him for his answer. Then he decided that he couldn't break his promise, so he asked the dragon's question.

The Wise Old Man said, "The dragon cannot fly because of the big diamond around his neck. He has to take it off." Again, the young man thanked the Wise Old Man. Then he left, without asking his own question.
On his way back home, he told the dragon what the Wise Old Man had said. "That's easy!" said the dragon. "Thank you! You can have the diamond, it might bring you luck." And he flew away. The young man took the diamond and went to the old woman's house. "Your daughter will smile when she meets the man she will marry," he said. At this moment, a very beautiful young woman came out of the house.
She took one look at the young man, and, ____________________, started to smile.
They got married soon afterwards.
The young man sold the dragon's diamond and was a very rich, very happy man for the rest of his life.

finally | immediately | it turned out that | unbelievably

Many years ago, a poor fisherman and his wife lived in a small house by the sea. The fisherman was happy, although he was poor, but his wife, unfortunately, wasn't. One day, the fisherman went fishing and caught a very big and beautiful fish. ______________________, the fish started talking to him. It said, "Please let me go. I'm an enchanted prince." The fisherman felt sorry for the fish and let it go.
When the fisherman went home and told the story to his wife, she was very angry because he had let the fish go without asking for something in return. She said to him, "Go back immediately and tell the fish I want a big house with a big garden and beautiful flowers!"

So the fisherman went back to the sea. The water had turned yellow. The fisherman was worried, but he shouted, "Fish of the sea, fish of the sea, I need your help so come to me." ______________________, the fish came and said, "What do you want?" The fisherman said, "My wife wants to have a big house with a big garden and flowers." "Go home and you will have what you want," said the fish and left.
When he got home, the fisherman couldn't believe his eyes: their house was big, with a big garden and lots of beautiful flowers.
"Are you happy now, wife?" the fisherman asked her. But all she said was, "We will see, we will see."

The next day, the fisherman's wife said to him, "Husband, we need a castle! Go back to the fish and tell him to give us one."
At first, the fisherman said, "Come on, wife! The fish will not give us a castle! He might get angry if I ask him for this!" "No, he surely won't!" said his wife. "And I want more: don't just ask him to give us a castle – tell him to give us the biggest castle in the world! And I want to be a queen! Go back immediately, and tell him this!"
So ______________________, the fisherman went back to the sea. The water had turned black. The fisherman was scared, but he shouted, "Fish of the sea, fish of the sea, I need your help so come to me!" The fish came and said, "What is it that you want?"

"My wife wants to be a queen, and she wants to live in the biggest castle in the world," the fisherman said. "Just go home," said the fish. "I have a surprise for your wife."
The fisherman was worried, but he decided to go home.
But what had happened to their home?! Unfortunately, the big house with the garden and the beautiful flowers had disappeared, and the little old house where they had always lived was there. His wife was sitting in the garden, crying. So in the end, ______________________ she had asked for too much and the fish had decided she did not deserve the favours it had given her.
The fisherman never saw the fish again, so they lived in the small old house until the end of their days.

Go for it! B1 Teacher's Resource Book | ISBN 978-3-19-032940-3 |

Use Unit 11, after classroom activity 2	**Activity** in pairs; role-play
Duration 15 mins.	**Focus** Adjectives describing emotions

Preparation

Make one copy of the worksheet for each student in your class. Bring enough dice to class (one for every pair of students).

Procedure

1. Inform students they are going to act out dialogues in roles and in specific moods.
2. Pair students up. Then hand out the worksheets. Explain to your students that they first have to complete the empty parts of the mood meter at the bottom with the adjectives given.
3. To start the activity, a student throws the dice and reads the corresponding situation on the "Act it out!" table. They then decide who will take which role in the dialogue. Then each of them throws the dice again and checks their mood meter: the adjective corresponding to the number on the dice will be the mood that they are in for their dialogue.
4. Students then improvise a dialogue in pairs. You can monitor and listen in, but since this is mostly a fun and fluency activity, error correction shouldn't be the most important part of it.

Extension

You can have a feedback round on the activity: what difficulties did students have when improvising the dialogue? Confident students can perform their dialogue in front of the class (and the class can guess the mood they were each in). Then all students can try the activity again with a different situation and different moods. Was it easier the second time around?

Act it out!

1 =	Your grandma gives you a handmade pullover for Christmas.
2 =	Your flight is delayed. Call your friend to tell him / her about it.
3 =	You lost your keys. Call your mother and ask her to bring her spare set of keys to your house.
4 =	Your neighbour is very loud.
5 =	Your wallet has been stolen. Talk to a police officer.
6 =	You are getting married. Talk to your mother about your decision.

The mood meter

optimistic disappointed delighted annoyed afraid angry

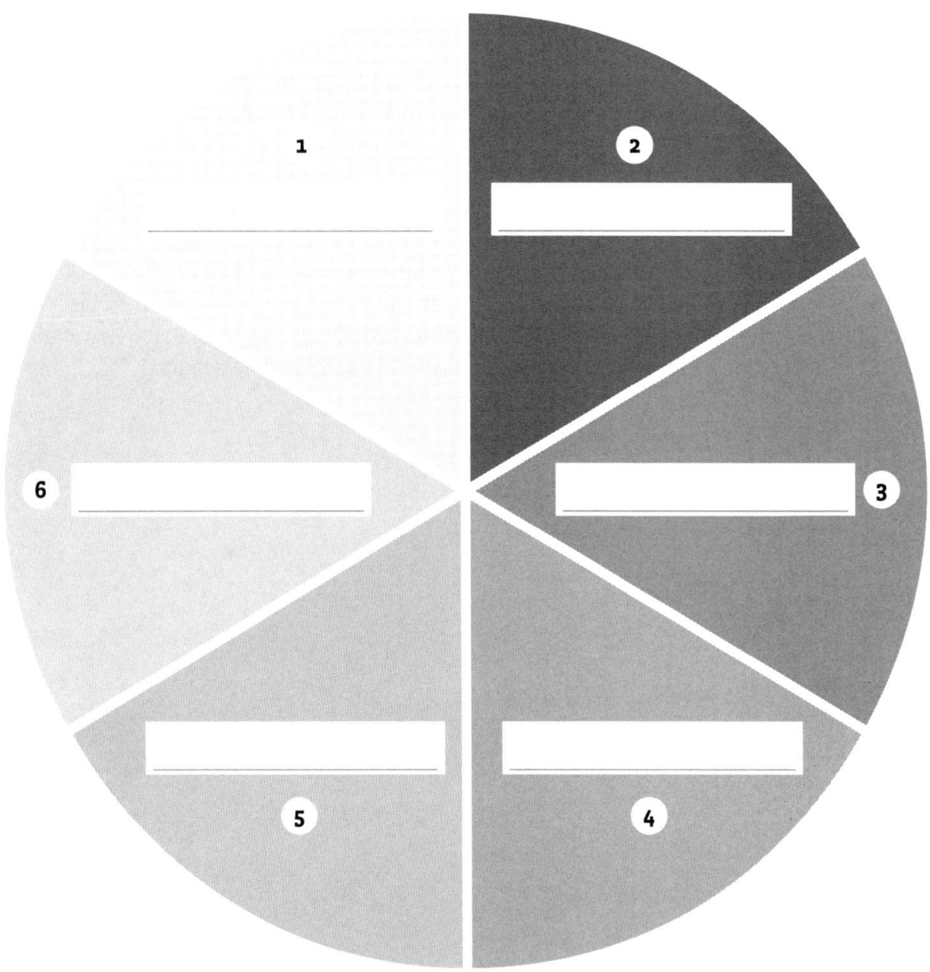

Go for it! B1 Teacher's Resource Book | ISBN 978-3-19-032940-3 | © 2018 Hueber Verlag

Use Unit 11, after classroom activity 4	**Activity** whole class; role-play
Duration 45 mins.	**Focus** *If* clause type 3; *I wish … / If only …* + past perfect

Preparation

Make one copy of the worksheet and cut it up.

Procedure

1. Write "couple problems" on the board and elicit some typical problems couples might have, e.g. argue about money, household tasks, etc. Make sure some typical expressions such as *cheat on someone*, *give someone attention*, or *split up* come up.
2. Make sure students have understood the use of the third conditional to express wishes and regrets about things that cannot be changed because they happened in the past. You can mention a typical sentence in an argument between couples, for example: *If you had (taken out the rubbish), I would have (made dinner)* or *I wish you hadn't (spent all day watching TV again).*
3. Set the scene: your students are on a reality TV show called *Couples Attack!* The guests to the show are couples who talk about their problems in front of a live audience. The audience can participate if they want, e. g. applaud, boo, or ask questions. Up to three pairs of students will represent the 'couples' on the show and act out an improvised dialogue in front of the class, who is the live audience. Place two chairs for the couple in front of the class, and one chair for the reality show host.
4. You will need up to three pairs / 'couples'; you can assign this role to students you know to be confident, or just ask for volunteers. Do the same with the host. You can either keep the same host for the complete activity or assign a new host for each pair. The class / audience will have to take part actively by asking questions, commenting, applauding, etc.
5. Hand out the role cards to the 'couples' and allow them about five minutes to prepare their roles and some things they want to say on the show. They should do this outside the classroom while you talk to the 'audience' and the 'host' and help them prepare their roles: the host will have to ask general questions such as *How long have you two been together?, What would you say is your biggest problem?, Why do you think he / she …?,* etc. The audience should try to think of some more questions they want to ask.
6. Once the 'couples' have prepared their performance, one of them comes to the front and the show starts. At the end, the audience decide if the couple should give their relationship another chance or split up. Then it's the next couple's turn.

Variation

If you have a strong class, you can try to incorporate the use of the second conditional for this activity, with sentences such as *If you didn't (watch TV all evening), I would (stay at home more to spend time with you).* Elicit some examples of the second conditional in Step 1 above (and illustrate the structure of the second conditional with chunks written on the board) and ask your 'couples' to use the second conditional as well. You could also ask the audience to give the couples advice during the show, for example saying *If I were you, I'd …*

Jonathan
You cheat on Mary because she spends too much time on social media and never has time for you. She loves the 'likes' that she gets from other men and women friends of hers – and you hate it! You want to end this.

Mary
You are spending so much time on social media because Jonathan doesn't give you enough attention. You want to go out with him, but he always works too much and is too tired to do anything when he comes home. And now you find out he is cheating on you!

Expressions to use
If you had / hadn't ..., I would / wouldn't have ...
I wish you had / hadn't ...
If only you had / hadn't ...

Sebastian
You are crazy about football. You watch football every Sunday and you like going to the stadium with friends, where you get drunk and celebrate after the game if your team wins. You sometimes have fights with the other teams' fans.

Larissa
You can't stand Sebastian's behaviour – he is an adult and he should stop acting like a child! You are almost convinced that you should split up, but friends told you to go to the show – this is your last try to save this relationship.

Expressions to use
If you had / hadn't ..., I would / wouldn't have ...
I wish you had / hadn't ...
If only you had / hadn't ...

Daniel
You are an artist and you work whenever you feel inspired. At times, when you are out with your girlfriend, Maria, you just get up and leave because you feel you have to be creative. You think Maria should understand you and not stand between you and your inspiration and your work. And she should stop seeing this other guy, Tom. You know what is going on between the two of them!

Maria
You can't believe that Daniel thinks you are cheating on him with Tom! You would never do that. Tom is just a friend, but he is a nice young man who shows interest in you – that's just what you need right now. You think you can't let Daniel do whatever he wants with you, for example leave you alone at a bar or a restaurant because he wants to go home and 'be creative'!

Expressions to use
If you had / hadn't ..., I would /wouldn't have ...
I wish you would / wouldn't ...
If only you had / hadn't ...

Go for it! B1 Teacher's Resource Book | ISBN 978-3-19-032940-3 |

Use	Activity
Unit 12, after classroom activity 3	in groups / whole class; role-play
Duration	**Focus**
20 mins.	Using *will* for predictions

Preparation

Photocopy the worksheet. You will divide the class into two groups; each group needs one worksheet. With a large class, you might need two worksheets per group for everyone to look at.

Procedure

1. Write the words "fortune teller" on the board and ask students if they know or can guess what a fortune teller does. Have they ever been to one, or do they know someone who has? Has anything predicted come true for them or that person?
2. Elicit some typical questions to or answers from a fortune teller and write them on the board (for example: *Will I get a better job? When will I meet the woman of my dreams? – The cards say you will. I can read in your hand that you won't. You will, but not soon*). Remind students that *will* is often used in this context to predict the future (refer them back to classroom activity 3e, where this function of *will* came up).
3. Divide your class into two (if possible, equal) groups. One group are the fortune tellers, the other ones are the clients.
4. Hand out the worksheets. Tell the clients to think about questions they would like to ask a fortune teller about the different topics / areas on the worksheet. Tell the fortune tellers to think about things they could predict about the different topics / areas. Students can use the prompts on the worksheets or their own ideas. They should each take some notes to use for the role-play.
5. Tell the fortune tellers to invent an unusual, exotic name for themselves (e.g. *Madame Futura*). They should sit in different corners of the classroom with a sheet of paper with the name hung above their heads or on the floor in front of them.
6. The clients walk around and ask their questions, and the fortune tellers make the predictions they've invented. Each client should talk to at least two fortune tellers.
7. Round up the activity with a short feedback session in plenary, e.g. *Timo, will something nice happen to you this year?*, or, *Anna, will you change your job soon?*

work (better position / new job / new boss / ...)	**travel** (destinations / adventures / new people / ...)
changes (learn something new / meet someone new / move to a new place / ...)	**self-fulfillment** (find the meaning of life / win an award / have a long life / ...)
love (meet someone / stay single / get married / ...)	**family** (start a family / have lots of children / have lots of grandchildren / ...)

Go for it! B1 Teacher's Resource Book | ISBN 978-3-19-032940-3 |

Use Unit 12, after classroom activity 3	**Activity** whole class; mingling
Duration 20 mins.	**Focus** Using *going to* for intentions

Preparation

Make one copy of the worksheet and cut up the cards. Each student in your class will receive one card. Bring some music on a CD or an MP3 player to class. Also bring a 'white elephant' type of item from home, e.g. an ugly item of clothing, a sick bag from an airplane, ...

Procedure

1. Give one student your white elepant item. Tell them enthusiastically that this is a gift for them and ask them what they are going to do with it. The student can give any answer, for example: *I'm going to sell it on eBay for 200 euros.* You can repeat this with other students. Try to be funny and enthusiastic about the gift to set a light, playful mood for the activity to follow, but also make sure students use *going to* in their answers to express their intentions.

2. Tell students that they are going to give some gifts to their classmates now. You are going to play some music and they are going to receive a card with an item on it. They walk around the classroom until the music stops, and then exchange their card with the person nearest to them at that point. When handing over the card, they should say something like, *This is for you! What are you going to do with it?* Receiving a gift, they should give a spontaneous answer (again, any funny or creative answer is fine; students can be imaginative).

3. Students then go on with their new card and give it to someone else, repeating the same question-answer sequence.

4. After students have talked to at least three other students, they go back to their seats and report to the class: Who gave the funniest answer? What gift(s) have they received and what are they going to do with them? For example, *I gave Timo a record player. He said he's going to put a vase with flowers on it. / Sarah gave me a candle. I'm going to use it to read the next time the electricity goes off.*

bowl of popcorn	aspirin	hammer
light bulb	old sofa	coffee machine
candle	vampire costume	envelope
earplugs	roller skates	eye mask
silver cutlery	hedgehog	funny hat
flowers	record player	mobile phone with broken display

Go for it! B1 Teacher's Resource Book | ISBN 978-3-19-032940-3 | © 2018 Hueber Verlag

Notes